ALZHEIMER'S

The Essential Guide

Need
— 2 —
Know

Jackie
Cosh

First published in Great Britain in 2009 by
Need2Know
Remus House
Coltsfoot Drive
Peterborough
PE2 9JX
Telephone 01733 898103
Fax 01733 313524
www.need2knowbooks.co.uk

Need2Know is an imprint of Forward Press Ltd.
www.forwardpress.co.uk
All Rights Reserved
© Jackie Cosh 2009
SB ISBN 978-1-86144-071-6
Cover photograph: Jupiter images

Contents

Introduction

An estimated that more than 400,000 people in the UK have Alzheimer's and this is set to double within a generation. But Alzheimer's affects many more people than these 400,000 sufferers. It affects the children of the sufferer, their spouse or partner and other family members as well as friends. It affects people who treat the person – whether for Alzheimer's or for indirect medical conditions. It affects the people who care for that person on a daily basis and those in regular contact with them.

This book can be used by all these people and anyone else with an interest in the disease. Many will want to learn all they can on the subject and some will want it in simple, easy to understand terms. The main focus, however, is primarily on the Alzheimer's sufferer and the questions posed which the newly diagnosed person, or even the undiagnosed person, will have.

Being diagnosed with Alzheimer's is life changing. At present there is no cure and the average progression of the condition takes eight to 12 years. While attitudes are changing towards Alzheimer's, the initial vision which springs to mind is likely to be a pretty negative one. However, as time goes on and developments are made in the area, the outlook is becoming increasingly more positive.

As well as attitudes changing, care and understanding are developing too. We now know more than ever before about the disease and how it affects the brain. We are in a better position to prepare for the progression and caregivers are better trained in providing medical attention and in helping sufferers live as full a life as possible. New drugs are coming out all the time and research is constantly underway to both find a cure and to better understand the disease.

Terry Pratchett did the condition a huge favour when he stood up and publicly admitted that he was in the early stages of Alzheimer's. By doing this, he made a statement – Alzheimer's is nothing to be ashamed of, it is a disease more and more of us are living with, not dying with.

'We now know more than ever before about the disease and how it affects the brain.'

I have made the assumption that if you're reading this book you're in the early stages of the disease, have either just been diagnosed or strongly suspect that this is what is going to be diagnosed. This is simply because, in my experience, this is when people are most eager for information on the subject and when they are looking to find out everything they can about Alzheimer's.

However, information is equally valid at different stages of the disease and helps you acknowledge the progression it will make, enabling you to plan ahead.

You will have many questions: why me? Is there anything I could have done to prevent it? What do I do now? How do I tell family and friends? These are likely to be your first thoughts and this book sets out to help you deal with them.

On a different level, other queries may come up: what's the difference between dementia and Alzheimer's? What does Alzheimer's actually do to the brain? What medication is available and what will it do?

Professionals working with people with Alzheimer's will also find this book informative. This includes nurses, care home staff, occupational therapists and anyone else working in a professional capacity.

The reasons people with Alzheimer's do certain things are often fascinating, although their actions may look as if they have no reason to them. For example, it may look as if the person has developed an aversion to potatoes and cauliflower, but research has uncovered that there are specific reasons for this. Understanding why can help with the professional care of the person.

Many of the questions addressed will also be ones which family and friends will have and this book is also written with these in mind. Chapters 9 and 10 take a specific focus on this.

The best way of coping with Alzheimer's is to approach it positively, not with fear. We have come a long way in the last 30 years and, with the research and development going on in the area, it cannot be ruled out that a cure may be found in our lifetime.

But whatever the future holds, a positive attitude can only really come from knowledge. This book will go a long way towards you gaining that knowledge, whether you or your partner suffer from the condition.

Disclaimer

This book is for general information on Alzheimer's and isn't intended to replace professional medical advice. If you suspect that you have Alzheimer's, it is important to consult a healthcare professional and obtain a proper diagnosis. If you have been diagnosed with Alzheimer's, you should follow the advice given to you by your GP and other healthcare professionals.

All the information in this book was correct at the time of going to press. National guidelines and recommendations can change, so it is important to check with your GP or healthcare professional before acting on any of the information in this book.

Chapter One

The Ghost of Alzheimer's Past

Hardly a week goes by without Alzheimer's being in the news – scientists discovering more about what causes it, developing a greater idea of how we can prevent or treat it, or another step being taken towards a cure.

It does seem to be a transient time for Alzheimer's and this becomes more apparent when you look back 20 or 30 years to what life used to be like for sufferers. We have come a long way from the days when little was known about Alzheimer's, when the attitude taken was that 'Granny's gone a bit mad' and when knowledge of how to help and make life easier for someone with the condition was practically non-existent.

What the perception used to be

As late as the 1950s, the general consensus was that all mental illness occurring in old age was due to senility, anxiety, depression, schizophrenia or more acute problems with cognitive functioning that would eventually evolve into dementia.

The diagnosis of Alzheimer's was usually made by ruling out other causes of dementia, such as syphilis, a brain tumour, alcoholism or a vitamin B12 deficiency, and it was usually made by a neurologist.

'It does seem to be a transient time for Alzheimer's and this becomes more apparent when you look back 20 or 30 years to what life used to be like for sufferers.'

Around 1980, the prevailing view of the conditions commonly known as 'degenerative dementia' was that they presented a hopeless picture. The care of such people was mainly based around dealing with their basic needs while letting the disease take its course. Little or no thought was put into keeping the mind active or into slowing the progess of the disease.

Even the terminologies surrounding dementia have changed over the last 50 years. 'Senile dementia' was a term often used 20 years ago and it was seen just as an accepted part of growing old.

What happened if you were diagnosed?

In the 1950s, no treatment was available and care was left to family members. For those who had no family support, there was the option of a mental hospital, but only if their behaviour was very disturbed and if they were really in no position to cook, clean and look after themselves. Even then it was a case of whether local psychiatrists could be persuaded to admit them.

In 1955, Martin Roth published a paper in which he detailed the outcomes after elderly people were admitted to stay at a mental hospital for two years. Those with symptoms of depression on admission were mostly already discharged after two years, while those diagnosed as schizophrenics were still hospitalised. Those categorised as 'dements' had mainly died, while those with acute confusional states had either recovered or died, with a 50/50 split on this.

Roth argued that it was likely that there was more than one outcome causing these various symptoms, and that only those with dementia symptoms had significant brain disease.

There was still a lot of guesswork going on and a lot of ignorance surrounding the disease. A fear of the unknown existed and, for the vast majority of the population, it was not a subject which was discussed. When it did occur, it tended to be hushed up and dealt with in the best way the family could.

When it changed

Roth's findings led eventually to a more positive attitude to Alzheimer's and slowly to psychogeriatric units being opened. In 1962, he opened a research unit which examined the relationship between physical disease and mental breakdown.

Dr Gary Blessed was recruited to examine the patients while hospitalised, establish a diagnosis and assess their cognitive functioning capability.

One of the things Blessed discovered was that Alzheimer's disease was the commonest pathology found, being responsible for 87% of cases. This led to the widespread belief that dementia in later life was always Alzheimer's. Research later proved this not to be true.

Even in the 1980s, the idea that psychotherapy could help people with dementia was quite foreign. It was assumed that people with Alzheimer's lacked the retentive powers of memory. But now several forms of therapeutic work are being explored and it has been discovered that people with dementia are far more resourceful than once thought.

How it has changed

The change has been gradual, with a growing awareness of the disease. In the 1970s and 1980s, specialist psychogeriatric units began to spring up all over the UK, but they were not universal. This led to an increase in numbers of specialists in this field (psychogeriatricians) and to the development within the Royal College of Psychiatrists of a group of such specialists who lobbied for improved diagnosis, treatment and management services for the elderly mentally ill. In many respects, the 1980s, are seen as a key decade in the history of Alzheimer's.

Old age psychiatry first became recognised in the 1980s but even in 1988, a year after one of the first public talks on the subject, Alzheimer's was still being described as the silent epidemic.

Slowly it became a subject people talked about and organisations like the Alzheimer's Society gave people a place they could turn to for advice and support. Research has now accelerated in a number of directions including that of drugs and diagnoses.

The increase in people living longer has resulted in Alzheimer's becoming an issue which cannot be ignored. Science and medicine may have been heading this way anyway, but the changes in demographics have certainly given it a helping hand.

What you can expect now

'The increase in people living longer has resulted in Alzheimer's becoming an issue which cannot be ignored. Science and medicine may have been heading this way anyway, but the changes in demographics have certainly given it a helping hand.'

So much has changed over the last 20 to 30 years, particularly since the 1980s. People are now being diagnosed much earlier, allowing more time to respond to drugs and treatment. As Alzheimer's is becoming more common and more is known about it, the stigma surrounding the disease is slowly disappearing. Alzheimer's is now being discussed instead of hushed up.

Long gone are the days when family care or a mental hospital were the only options for sufferers. The specialist psychogeriatric units which began to spring up in the 1970s and 1980s have now been replaced by specialist nursing homes.

Alzheimer's is no longer viewed as an inevitable part of old age and efforts are being made to learn more about how to prevent and treat it. While the money invested is still not enough, it does signify a big change in attitudes, and progress is being made.

Falls are the most frequent and serious type of accident in the over 65s and are a common problem in people in the later stages of Alzheimer's. Help the Aged have started a National Falls Awareness Day, helping to raise national recognition of this problem.

Attitudes from medical professionals, in particular GPs, are slowly but surely changing as knowledge is greater. Some people were being misdiagnosed 25 years ago and GPs only really diagnosed it in the later stages when symptoms were very obvious and sufferers were becoming unmanageable for family and friends. GPs are now able to diagnose at an earlier stage when help can be given and plans can be made.

In December 2008, the government announced that all NHS GPs in England would receive training on how to recognise the early symptoms of Alzheimer's. When surveyed, only 31% said they felt that they had received adequate training to diagnose and manage the disease themselves.

Such action should lead to GPs being better placed to refer patients on to organisations which can help and provide support. Though help is out there, it is unusual for GPs to pass details to patients, and Alzheimer's organisations receiving requests from GPs for more information on what they can provide is still a rare occurrence.

Case studies

Alzheimer's in the early 1980s

Cathy's mum was diagnosed with Alzheimer's in 1981 aged 66.

'We first noticed changes in my mum about 1979. She ran a small business and we were becoming increasingly concerned about her. She was having problems handling money, had developed a lack of reasoning and judgement and was doing things out of character.

'After many visits to the GP, he finally diagnosed it as an old war wound from when she had been hit by the bombings in the war. He said it was just part of old age.

'Even when it was eventually diagnosed, I wasn't told and my mother kept it hidden from me. At one visit to the GP, the receptionist said, "It's a shame about your mum isn't it?" When I questioned her on what was wrong with my mum, she backtracked.

'Things got so bad that her GP did admit to me that it was dementia. "Pleasantly confused" was how he put it and "all part of old age". I was accused of covering up for her by doing her hair and making sure she was well presented. I was told this stopped them from doing an accurate assessment of her and that it would be better if I would leave her to her own devices so they could section her under the Mental Health Act.'

When hospital care did come, it was not the end of the problems. Cathy's mother walked out of the psychiatric hospital in her slippers before it was decided to transfer her to somewhere more secure. Several health problems were misdiagnosed, with Cathy being told she was overreacting, and staff appeared ignorant of her mother's needs and lacked sensitivity.

'When surveyed, only 31% [of GPs] said they felt that they had received adequate training to diagnose and manage the disease themselves.'

Care did eventually improve and her mum did settle, but it was a long, hard struggle for the family.

Alzheimer's in the 2000s

Sadie, 75, was diagnosed with Alzheimer's two years ago.

'It was in 1990 when I started to have word finding difficulties. At this time I was working as a lecturer in a college of education. I was used to doing a lot of public speaking and was increasingly forgetting words and phrases. Meanwhile, I had been elected as a local authority councillor and my symptoms were becoming more apparent.

'By the time I went to the doctor's two years ago, the problems had been going on for so long that I had got used to people not believing me. He referred me to a neurologist, a psychiatrist and a psychologist, and following three different types of brain scan, a diagnosis of Alzheimer's was made.

'I was shocked. I hadn't expected it even though I had felt it in my bones. Since then I have tried two different types of drugs but unfortunately they didn't agree with me.

'I did get to a point soon after diagnosis when I was told that there was nothing else to be done for me. That really hit me very hard and I felt dumped by the system. Then, luckily, a neighbour told me about Alzheimer's Scotland and that made a big difference. Through that contact I was put in touch with the Scottish Dementia Working Group. Both have been fantastic. They have given me all sorts of books and information. They have explained things to me and told me where to go for help. They visit me at home and I know I can call them if I need to.

'I have managed to adapt my life to make things easier for me. I will now ask people for help more. Most importantly, I continue to enjoy my life socialising with friends.'

Summing Up

- Although today we may still have a long wish list for the treatment of people with Alzheimer's, including improvements in diagnosis, care and long term treatment, we have come a long way from the attitudes in the 1950s when Alzheimer's was seen as inevitable.

- This is seen in the changes in terminology used. It is now rare to hear the phrases 'degenerative dementia' or 'senile dementia'.

- As recent as 1980, the view of Alzheimer's sufferers was that there was nothing that could be done for them apart from dealing with their basic needs.

- Dr Gary Blessed and Dr Martin Roth conducted significant research in this area, with their research findings leading to more being known about Alzheimer's and a change in attitudes.

- The 1980s is a key decade. For the first time, elderly mental health became a branch of the Royal College of Psychiatrists in its own right.

- As mental hospitals have shut, more specialist care homes have sprung up and the stigma surrounding Alzheimer's is no longer so prevalent.

- Much has been achieved but many people still feel that they are abandoned following diagnosis. The introduction of more relevant training for GPs should go some way towards ending that.

'Although today we may still have a long wish list for the treatment of people with Alzheimer's, including improvements in diagnosis, care and long term treatment, we have come a long way.'

Chapter Two

What is Alzheimer's?

The terms Alzheimer's and dementia are used interchangeably to such an extent that many people consider them to mean the same thing. To the outsider looking at the symptoms and development, they may appear the same. But at this stage it is useful to explain what the differences are and how the two are connected.

Medical definition

Alzheimer's disease is a form of dementia. It's the most common form, affecting more than 400,000 people in the UK and accounting for about two thirds of cases of dementia. Dementia is an umbrella term to describe a serious deterioration in mental function such as memory, language, orientation and judgement.

It is estimated that there are between 50 and 100 types of dementia. The second most common is vascular dementia (also known as multi-infarct dementia), followed by dementia with Lewy bodies and fronto-temporal dementia. Increasingly, Korsakoff's syndrome (alcohol related dementia) is being seen as the effects of binge drinking take their toll.

So it is quite understandable that people will get the terms dementia and Alzheimer's mixed up. The majority of people will meet someone who has a form of dementia and will have no need to distinguish what type it is. The symptoms are similar and much of the advice given with regards to Alzheimer's is valid for other forms of dementia.

But in order to understand more about Alzheimer's and how it affects us, it is useful to understand how Alzheimer's differs from other forms of dementia, how it affects the brain and why certain changes occur.

'Alzheimer's disease is a form of dementia. It's the most common form, affecting more than 400,000 people in the UK and accounting for about two thirds of cases of dementia.'

A short history lesson

To understand more about the disease, we will begin with a short history lesson on how Alzheimer's was first discovered.

Alzheimer's is named after the German psychiatrist and neuropathologist Dr Alois Alzheimer. During his work at the start of the 20th century, he became fascinated by a patient in her fifties who showed signs of short term memory loss and other behavioural symptoms. When she died in 1906, he had her medical notes and brain sent to his lab.

'Alzheimer's is named after the German psychiatrist and neuropathologist Dr Alois Alzheimer... He became fascinated by a patient in her fifties who showed signs of short term memory loss and other behavioural symptoms.'

Along with two Italian colleagues, he examined the brain and discovered that it had decreased in size. This was due to a large number of nerve cells dying. Under the microscope he saw unusual plaques which were partly made up of brain cells and tangles inside the dying cells. On 3 November 1906, Alzheimer presented a key paper at the South West German Society of Alienists. Within five years his research findings were being used to diagnose patients outside Germany.

Over the first few decades of the 20th century, Alzheimer's was largely ignored. But in the 1970s scientists found that certain areas of the brain were shrinking more than others and that particular types of nerve cells, the temporal lobes at the side of the brain which are important in storing recent memories, were more damaged.

What the difference is

Many of the symptoms you may experience will be similar to those of most types of dementia, but there are some differences and it is worth noting these. To understand better, here are some brief details on the main types of dementia other than Alzheimer's:

- **Vascular dementia** occurs when blood vessels are damaged, affecting oxygen supply to the brain. This can cause brain cells to die, leading to a series of mini strokes. Often, these strokes are so slight that they may not be noticed, but each stroke destroys a small number of brain cells by cutting off its blood supply. Eventually this may cause vascular dementia. With vascular dementia, mental decline is likely to have a clear start date, often a stroke (also known as a cerebral vascular accident or a CVA) and symptoms tend to get worse in a series of steps rather than a gradual decline. Because some areas of the brain may be more affected than others, sufferers may have some symptoms but not others. Symptoms may include depression, mood swings and epilepsy. Vascular dementia and Alzheimer's disease often occur together.

- **Dementia with Lewy bodies** is so called after the abnormal collection of proteins called Lewy bodies that can occur in the nerve cells of the brain. It affects concentration, attention, memory and language, as well as the ability to judge distances and to reason. Visual hallucinations are another side effect and more than half of people with Lewy bodies develop symptoms of Parkinson's disease.

- **Fronto-temporal dementia** tends to begin at an earlier age than Alzheimer's disease, usually in a person in their forties or fifties. It is so called because the frontal lobe of the brain is affected. Like Alzheimer's disease, it involves a progressive decline in a person's mental abilities over the years, but damage to the brain cells is more localised than in Alzheimer's and the sufferer does not usually have lapses in memory. Because the frontal lobe of the brain controls behaviour and mood, people with fronto-temporal dementia may become fixed in their moods, often appearing selfish and uncaring.

- **Korsakoff's syndrome** is alcohol-related dementia. People with Korsakoff's are usually deficient in thiamine (vitamin B1), often due to poor diet. The main symptom is short term memory loss but the person may also have difficulties in learning new skills.

How Alzheimer's affects the brain

Alzheimer's is caused by plaques and tangles developing in the brain, leading to the death of brain cells and a shortage of brain chemicals which are involved in transmitting messages within the brain. The plaques and tangles then start to attack other connections between brain cells, making the condition worse.

Why certain changes occur

One of the most commonly mentioned symptoms of Alzheimer's is memory loss – usually short term memory. It isn't known why this is but it is thought that long term memories are stored in a different part of the brain and are relearned many times, making them more stable.

As more nerve cells die, the brain starts to shrink. It is this decrease in size which first caught Dr Alois Alzheimer's attention all those years ago. As the brain starts to shrink and it has to rely on fewer chemical messengers, key mental skills start to diminish.

Changes to expect

'One of the most commonly mentioned symptoms of Alzheimer's is memory loss – usually short term memory.'

As the disease progresses, memory loss is likely to become worse, progressing from occasional short term memory loss to more regular memory loss and eventually loss of longer term memory.

Symptoms may include mood swings, forgetting recent events, names and faces, becoming confused when handling money or driving a car and problems with language. Wandering off and a loss of inhibitions are common symptoms in the advanced stages.

Summing Up

▪ Alzheimer's is one of the five most common types of dementia. The other types include vascular, Lewy bodies, fronto-temporal dementia and Korsakoff's.

▪ The disease was discovered by German psychiatrist and neuropathologist Dr Alois Alzheimer.

▪ The symptoms of Alzheimer's are caused by plaques and tangles in the brain which kill off brain cells and reduce its size.

▪ As the disease progresses, key brain functions will deteriorate.

Chapter Three

Signs

The time from first symptom to diagnosis can be a journey in itself, and many years may pass from the time you, or friends and family, notice that something is amiss. A poll conducted by researchers Millward Brown in 2004 found that out of six European countries, the UK has, on average, the longest time between first symptoms being noticed and a diagnosis of Alzheimer's being made (32 months). The average time across Germany, France, Italy, Spain and Poland was 18 months.

Why the delay in diagnosis?

The 32 months in the UK compared to 18 elsewhere is some difference, so why is there such a delay here in Britain? The researchers suggested that the delay could be down to the reluctance of many people to make a fuss about symptoms, choosing to ignore them and hoping they will go away.

There is also the theory that the early symptoms of Alzheimer's can often signify something else. It is a hard disease to diagnose and we tend to assume that we will become more forgetful as we get older. The problem is determining when the forgetfulness is just part of getting older and when it is a sign that something more serious is wrong.

Experts do agree that treatment for Alzheimer's is most effective if it begins in the early stages. But what are the early symptoms? How do you know that it is Alzheimer's?

'A poll conducted by researchers Millward Brown in 2004 found that out of six European countries, the UK has, on average, the longest time between first symptoms being noticed and a diagnosis of Alzheimer's being made.'

First symptoms of Alzheimer's

As stated previously, part of the reason diagnosis takes so long is due to the fact that the symptoms can often be mistaken for something else. Symptoms may initially be so subtle that they are not noted.

It is usually best to rule out other conditions first such as depression or a urinary tract infection (UTI). Both conditions can result in forgetfulness and, at times, a confused state. It should also be noted how long the symptoms have been going on for and if they have been getting worse.

While symptoms can vary between individuals, a diagnosis of Alzheimer's will involve looking for the most common early symptoms.

'Forgetfulness is probably the most well known of the first symptoms of Alzheimer's and fits in with the stereotypical image people have of sufferers.'

- Forgetfulness
  This is probably the most well known of the first symptoms of Alzheimer's and fits in with the stereotypical image people have of sufferers. In the early stages, it is short term memory as opposed to long term memory which is affected – forgetting what you did yesterday or going upstairs for something and then forgetting why you were going up. Long term events and childhood memories appear to be stored in a different part of the brain and tend to stay for longer.

- Mixing up words
  From time to time, all of us begin sentences and then forget what we were going to say, but sometimes there can be signs that it is more than this. It may at first appear to be forgetfulness but over time will be more demonstrative of a lack of coherency, with cognitive functions starting to become impaired.

- Getting times, places and people mixed up
  This is often the symptom which is the trigger for action to be taken. In the early stages, this may be as simple as going to an appointment on the wrong day or perhaps turning up more than once. Slightly later on it could involve going back to an old house, perhaps a childhood home, or getting family members mixed up – recognising a daughter but thinking she is the mother.

- Difficulty performing familiar tasks
  Household tasks may become a problem. Tasks which have been

performed for years such as putting on the washing machine may slide from the memory. You may begin to have difficulty with money and lose the ability to know how much to hand over in shops.

- **Changes in personality**
  Often, this symptom shows in ways nobody can pinpoint. You may become anxious, changing from being a calm and collected person to becoming an anxious one. Feelings of paranoia may appear and inhibitions may come out in inappropriate ways.

- **Change in mood or behaviour**
  This is a symptom which is often misdiagnosed. You can become depressed and may at first be diagnosed with depression, when in fact the depression is a symptom of something more serious.

- **Misplacing things**
  You may notice that you start putting objects in the fridge which shouldn't go there or hiding things all over the house for no apparent reason.

- **Listlessness**
  This is also a symptom of depression but, again, may be a sign of something more serious. If a previously active person starts to spend hours in front of the TV and gives up on old hobbies, it is worth investigating further.

How Alzheimer's develops

This section is harder to write. Unlike the early symptoms, there are no guides on how the disease will develop. We do know that Alzheimer's is characterised by a more steady decline than other forms of dementia where the person's health may drop in stages, but nobody can give a timescale or foresee what the future holds. This can be frustrating as comfort can be gained from knowing what to expect.

What is known is that everyone develops at different speeds. Some people may stay at the same stage for a long time, others may go downhill rapidly. The earlier the diagnosis, the higher the chance of more being done to slow the progress. Drugs may be tried and activities may be organised to keep the brain active.

Other signs that it is progressing

There are signs that the disease is progressing. Perhaps the tasks which you could previously perform a few months ago are no longer within your abilities. Friends and family sometimes first notice that symptoms have worsened when the person begins to revert back to the past, thinking today is yesteryear. Forgetting to take medication and unusual weight loss are two further symptoms. Weight loss could be a symptom of Alzheimer's when someone is eating sufficiently but still losing weight. However, it could also be a sign of not eating properly or of forgetting how to cook.

When to see a doctor or specialist

'Your GP is a good starting point as they are likely to be the best point of contact for accessing services.'

The answer here is to see someone as early as possible. If you have a hunch that something just isn't right, or if family and friends have started to notice and point things out, it is time to seek advice.

Your GP is a good starting point as they are likely to be the best point of contact for accessing services. Many people are surprised at how little is done by the GP. The GP might say it looks like dementia after ruling out other causes such as a urinary tract infection (UTI), depression, chest infection or anything where your body is full of toxins. But from there they really need something to work on in order to take action – a problem connected to Alzheimer's which needs dealing with.

If there are problems with behaviour, like aggression, a referral can be made to a psychiatrist. If help is needed with daily needs, social workers may become involved. However, if the Alzheimer's is not causing any problems, the GP is unlikely to suggest action.

Treatment and diagnosis of Alzheimer's is advancing all the time but even today it is likely that any diagnosis of Alzheimer's will not be made with certainty. Brain scans are not routinely performed and a diagnosis will usually be given based on behaviour and changes over time.

Questions to ask

Most of the questions which immediately come into your mind cannot be answered: why me? How long will I go on like this? When will it get worse? How long do I have? A GP can't answer these questions, although it is understandable that you will want to know.

After the initial questions come the practical questions: what do I do now? How can I keep as well as possible? Now is the time to ask about medication and its benefits as most drugs are most effective earlier on. It is also worth asking about local services and what is available to help you keep your brain active, such as mind clinics, support groups and daycare.

It really is worth emphasising here that, more often than not, GPs will not be the best sources of information. This may begin to change soon but questions are better directed at specialists in social work, psychiatry or in any of the organisations mentioned overleaf. The information is there and help is available.

What will happen following diagnosis?

This really does vary depending on whether it is viewed that there is a need for further help or not. If it is considered that further health or social work services are required, a needs assessment may be carried out in the home by either a social worker or a community psychiatric nurse (CPN). The idea of the needs assessment is to gather as much information as possible in order to make a decision.

The questions asked will be thorough and will go through all aspects of your daily living skills: how you get about, whether you socialise much, if you wear glasses, if you need to see a chiropodist, if you have any problems with incontinence, if you are able to wash yourself and if you have any other physical ailments.

The assessment is often very long and goes through all aspects of your whole self – everything you do during the day and if you need any help, what services you need and any aids or adaptations you may need in your home. The idea is that it should flag up any problem areas.

'If it is considered that further health or social work services are required, a needs assessment may be carried out in the home by either a social worker or a community psychiatric nurse.'

Other areas of help

Once a diagnosis has been made, you will of course be looking for areas of help. These come in various forms.

Daycare centres

These are usually run by the local health board, usually requiring a social worker or GP referral. The set up varies but the aims are the same: to encourage activities which keep the mind active and to allow further assessment should it be required.

Beginning with a morning snack and drink, the day is then filled with various group activities: discussing current news events, card making, general knowledge quizzes, ball games for coordination, basic colouring in, baking groups, reminiscence boxes and group discussions where everyone is given the opportunity to talk about their favourite holidays, where they went to school or anything else about the past. There is plenty to do and you get to pick and choose what you get involved in.

Support groups

These are informal sessions which usually happen once a month and are often run by groups such as Alzheimer's Scotland or the Alzheimer's Society. Here you can meet with others in the same situation, talk about your worries, share experiences and discuss how to deal with things. As well as being useful for sharing information on local services and what there is available, it is also good to know that there are other people out there in the same boat as you.

Home visits

Home visits are conducted depending on the individual's needs. Social workers may visit regularly (if they feel you need it) and care workers may be assigned to help you with daily needs. CPNs may come out in the short term if it is felt that help is needed with anxiety, behaviour or depression.

'As well as being useful for sharing information on local services and what there is available, it is also good to know that there are other people out there in the same boat as you.'

The Alzheimer's Society and Alzheimer's Scotland

These two organisations have been left until last but it is certainly not because of their lesser importance. Many people with Alzheimer's describe them as lifesavers, providing help, advice and the support that is often lacking elsewhere. They can provide information and leaflets on various aspects of the disease and give advice on what help there is available, as well as providing valuable services like support groups, drop in cafes and befrienders. See the help list at the back of the book for contact details.

'The Alzheimer's Society and Alzheimer's Scotland have been left until last but it is certainly not because of their lesser importance. Many people with Alzheimer's describe them as lifesavers, providing help, advice and the support that is often lacking elsewhere.'

Summing Up

- The earlier a diagnosis is made, the more effective treatment will be.

- While symptoms do vary, there are several common first symptoms.

- Your GP should be the first port of call who can rule out other causes of your symptoms in the first instance.

- Services are only usually offered if it is felt that there is a problem which needs to be treated.

- Support and help is available but it may not be offered initially. The Alzheimer's Society and Alzheimer's Scotland are great for everything from information to regular support.

Chapter Four

Can I Prevent the Disease from Getting Worse?

Following diagnosis, one of the first questions often asked is what can be done to stop the onset and can it be cured? It is only natural that you will be looking for a cure or some way of preventing the disease from worsening.

Millions of pounds are spent each year researching Alzheimer's and its causes and possible cures. However, it is argued that there is still not enough being invested. However, progress is being made and it is possible that we are just one step away from discovering a cure.

But whether a cure is found in the near future or not, we need to look at other issues – namely lifestyle. Lifestyle can play a big part in how the disease progresses. Having an active social life and keeping mentally and physically fit keeps the brain cells alive and can go a long way in slowing down the hold Alzheimer's has on the brain.

Research conducted in 2002 by Dr Linda Clare from University College London found that memory training can help some early-stage Alzheimer's patients. It is thought that the memory games work by slowly re-establishing links in the language-controlling areas of the brain. More details can be found on the website of the American Psychological Association, www.apa.org/releases/memory_training.html, or on the website of *The Lancet* at www.thelancet.com.

Other studies have found that it is the variety of leisure and physical activities rather than the frequency or intensity which is more important.

'Lifestyle can play a big part in how the disease progresses. **Having an active social life and keeping mentally and physically fit keeps the brain cells alive and can go a long way in slowing down the hold Alzheimer's has on the brain.'**

Anti-dementia drugs

While as yet no drugs can provide a cure for the disease, there are drugs available which can improve the symptoms and help slow down progression. There is also evidence that these drugs should be started in the early stages when they have more effect.

There are two main types of anti-dementia drugs that are used for people with Alzheimer's.

Acetylcholinesterase inhibitors

'While as yet no drugs can provide a cure for the disease, there are drugs available which can improve the symptoms and help slow down progression.'

Research tells us that the brains of people with Alzheimer's show a loss of nerve cells that use a chemical messenger called acetylcholine. The more nerve cells that are lost, the more severe the symptoms people experience.

The inhibitors prevent the enzyme acetylcholinesterase from breaking down acetylcholine in the brain. Increasing concentration of acetylcholine leads to increased communication between the nerve cells which use acetylcholine as a chemical messenger, which in turn can improve or stabilise symptoms.

Between 40-60% of people with Alzheimer's will benefit from taking one of these drugs. At present in the UK, they are only licensed for use by people with mild to moderate Alzheimer's, although several studies have found that they do improve the symptoms of people with severe Alzheimer's.

According to an Alzheimer's Society survey of 4,000 people, sufferers using these drugs report increases in motivation and confidence, reduction in anxiety and improvement in memory and thinking.

There are three brands of acetylcholinesterase inhibitors:

- Aricept (donepezil hydrochloride).
- Exelon (rivastigmine).
- Reminyl (galantamine).

Aricept

Aricept (donepezil hydrochloride) is manufactured by a company called Eisai and was the first Alzheimer's drug to be licensed in the UK. Studies have found that it reduces hallucinations and behavioural problems and improves cognition and function in some people. People tend to find that it improves their condition or at least stabilises it.

Possible side effects: everyone is different and will, to an extent, react differently. Some reported side effects include fatigue, vomiting, stomach cramps, diarrhoea, nausea, headaches, loss of appetite and difficulty sleeping.

Exelon

Exelon (rivastigmine) was the second Alzheimer's drug to be licensed in the UK and is made by Novartis Pharmaceutical. Studies have found that it has a positive effect on cognition. One such study found that people with Alzheimer's disease who had high blood pressure gained more from the drug than people without high blood pressure.

Possible side effects: nausea, vomiting, loss of appetite and weight loss can occur but are more likely when the drug is first taken and may settle down in time. To prevent such side effects it is best to take with a meal.

Reminyl

Reminyl (galantamine) originates from the bulbs of snowdrops and narcissi and was the third drug to be licensed in the UK. It was co-developed by Shire Pharmaceuticals and the Janssen Research Foundation and was launched in September 2000.

Research has found that Reminyl is effective in maintaining cognition and that it improves behaviour and functional ability.

Possible side effects: nausea and vomiting sometimes occur when first taking Reminyl but this often settles down in time. Other potential side effects are diarrhoea, indigestion, decreased appetite, weight loss, headache, dizziness, tiredness, sleepiness and sleeplessness.

Ebixa (memantine)

Ebixa works differently from the acetylcholinesterase inhibitors. It blocks the neurotransmitter glutamate, a chemical messenger in the brain which is released in excessive quantities when brain cells are damaged by Alzheimer's. Glutamate is involved in normal memory and learning processes. By blocking the release of excess glutamate, it protects the brain from cell degeneration.

Launched in October 2002, it is the first drug to be licensed for treatment in people with moderate to severe Alzheimer's. It is not routinely used in the NHS because it is thought that the benefits are too small to be cost-effective. However NICE (the National Institute for Health and Clinical Excellence) has recommended further research on the drug.

Because the other drugs are for people in the mild to moderate stages of the disease, they are likely to have been stopped before Ebixa is started. However, according to research conducted in the US, combining Ebixa with Aricept has proved to be more effective than using them on their own.

Studies have also found that patients who take Ebixa experience significant benefits in memory, language and the ability to perform daily activities. It has also been found that in people in the mid to later stages of the disease it can help with aggression and irritation, and can temporarily slow down the progression of symptoms, including those of everyday functions. However, the effect depends on the individual and others may not notice any difference.

Possible side effects: dizziness, headaches, tiredness and increased blood pressure can occur but these are likely to settle down over time. Ebixa is not recommended for people with severe kidney problems because this group have not been tested.

It is worth noting that none of the above drugs have been found to be addictive.

Other drugs

While those just listed are the drugs available to deal directly with the disease, Alzheimer's sufferers are likely to experience symptoms which other drugs may help with. There is as likely a chance, if not more of a chance, of being on other medication, so it is worth finding out about other drugs.

It must be noted that the following drugs are not universally used by everyone – they will be prescribed for certain symptoms. They are certainly not used by all sufferers of Alzheimer's but they may become an option at some point, so it is certainly a good idea to understand what they are and what they are used for. Remember to always get professional medical advice from your GP.

Antipsychotics or neuroleptics

Antipsychotics and neuroleptics are commonly used for restlessness, aggression and psychotic symptoms in people with dementia. About 60% of nursing home patients take them, normally people in the more severe stage of the disease. Commonly used drugs in this category include trazodone, quetiapine and haloperidol. In the short term, clinical trials have found that they can reduce aggression and, to a certain extent, psychotic symptoms. In the long term, the benefits are limited.

Anti-convulsants and antidepressants

Anti-convulsant drugs such as sodium vaproate and carbamazepine, and antidepressants such as trazodone and citalopram, are also sometimes used to reduce aggression and for seizures.

The anti-dementia drug memantine may also be effective in treating aggression and other symptoms of agitation.

Depression is common in Alzheimer's sufferers. In the early stages, this may be largely due to a reaction to the diagnosis as you attempt to come to terms with the disease. But it may also be a result of reduced chemical transmitters in the brain.

Alternative medicine

As with any disease, many people will look to alternative and natural medicine in the hope of being able to treat the disease with fewer side effects. Alzheimer's is no different and there are several natural products and foods which help relieve symptoms, some with more evidence to support them than others.

Gingko biloba

Gingko biloba comes from the maidenhair tree and has long been believed to enhance memory. More than one in 10 dementia sufferers takes the herb at some point. It is thought that gingko biloba increases blood flow to the brain. It also acts as an antioxidant and some studies have found it to be nearly as effective as cholinesterase inhibitors.

'One of the most commonly mentioned symptoms of Alzheimer's is memory loss – usually short term memory.'

But the jury is still out on gingko biloba and whether it works for relieving Alzheimer's symptoms. A study published in 1997 in the *Journal of the American Medical Association* found that, in some participants, a modest improvement in cognition, eating, dressing and social behaviour was reported.

However, another similar sized study published in 2008 by the Alzheimer's Society suggested that people may be wasting their time taking the herb. It found that the herb had no significant impact on the mental function or quality of life of Alzheimer's sufferers and did not prevent symptoms from getting worse.

For people who do wish to give it a try, few side effects are noted but it can delay blood clotting and should not be used by people with bleeding disorders or people taking anticoagulants.

Vitamin E

Vitamin E is found in soya beans, sunflower seeds, corn, wholegrain foods, fish liver oils and nuts. Studies have found that it can slow the progress of Alzheimer's disease. A study reported in the *Archives of Neurology* (published by the American Medical Association) found that people aged 65 to 102 who ate fish at least once a week over the study's three or more years showed

35% less decline in cognitive functioning than those who didn't take it. It can, however, interfere with blood clotting and should not be consumed in large doses. Some experts recommend no more than two units a day.

Lemon balm

Lemon balm has been used as a mild sedative for years. It is thought to reduce anxiety, stress and sleep disorders. Several small studies have also found that lemon balm improves memory and appears to increase the activity of the chemical messenger acetylcholine.

Other treatments

As stated earlier, there are alternatives to drugs, particularly in the early stages. Many of these are based on changing behaviours.

Reality orientation therapy

Reality orientation therapy is based on the belief that if you continually tell or show certain reminders to people with mild to moderate memory loss, it will result in an increase in interaction with others and will improve orientation.

It can be taught to the family or caregivers by a psychotherapist and is best performed in the home with plenty of familiar objects surrounding the sufferer. Every conversation should include the time of day, day of the week and mention of familiar objects and people.

Art therapy

Research conducted at the University of Sussex and Goldsmiths College, London, found that half of Alzheimer's sufferers who took part in a 10 week art therapy course showed significant improvement in their symptoms. They became more relaxed, more sociable and their depression scores reduced. Other research has backed this theory up and it certainly fits in with the advice to keep active.

'Research conducted at the University of Sussex and Goldsmiths College, London, found that half of Alzheimer's disease sufferers who took part in a 10 week art therapy course showed significant improvement in their symptoms.'

Summing Up

- Treatment in the early stages may or may not involve drugs.

- There are several anti-dementia drugs out there, so if one doesn't suit you it is likely that another will. Most of these drugs work best in the early stages of the disease.

- There are also several drugs on hand for the various symptoms.

- Research has found that alternative medicine can play a big part, with research constantly discovering new ways of dealing with the disease.

- Most of all, keeping fit and active will go a long way to slowing down the progression of the disease.

Chapter Five

Why Me?

Why me? It's a question you are likely to ask. Why me and not the next person? Did I do something to bring this on? Could I have done anything to prevent getting Alzheimer's? When you are first diagnosed with Alzheimer's, lots of thoughts go round in your head as you try to make sense of the situation.

Have I done something to cause it?

It is easy to look back at your life and wonder if there was something you did or some aspect of your life that caused or made you more prone to the disease. In many ways, reading the latest research in the national press only makes things worse. Barely a month goes by without at least one of the daily newspapers reporting the latest research and the latest possibilities of what causes the condition.

But these reports must be put into perspective. The whole world is keen to find out what causes it so steps can be taken to prevent it. A breakthrough may come tomorrow, it may come in 20 years time. Whenever it does, it's likely that some of the many pieces of research being conducted will have played their part and will have helped push the researchers in the right direction, or at least steered them away from the wrong direction.

The truth is, of the most common types of dementia, Alzheimer's is probably one of the hardest for which to pin down a cause. While vascular dementia has been linked to diet and in particular high blood pressure, heart problems, high cholesterol and diabetes, and Korsakoff's is strongly linked to excessive alcohol consumption, less is known about what causes Alzheimer's.

The most obvious thing you have done is get older – obviously something none of us can help. Your chances of developing Alzheimer's increases as you get older, but there are still an estimated 15,000 younger people (under 65s) in the UK with the disease.

From what we have learnt so far and from research conducted on other forms of dementia and conditions affecting the brain, it is likely that lifestyle and environmental factors play a big part. It has been suggested that keeping the brain active by regularly doing crosswords and puzzles can lower your risk, as can eating a healthy diet rich in omega 3 fatty acids. A connection has also been made with previous head injuries.

'Your chances of developing Alzheimer's increases as you get older, but there are still an estimated 15,000 younger people (under 65s) in the UK with the disease.'

Is it because I did ...?

One negative result of the almost weekly news of research into causes of Alzheimer's is that we feel compelled to search for an explanation for us developing the condition. It seems as if there must be an explanation out there and that something we have done in the past must have caused it.

However, at this point in time we can't tell for sure what has caused it and focusing on it is not constructive and won't get you anywhere. But this doesn't stop you thinking.

There are several theories and possible causes that have now been ruled out. The most common is probably aluminium – for years this was topped as being a possible cause. This theory has been around for more than 40 years and, despite numerous pieces of research, a direct link has yet to be found. Some studies have found higher than average levels of aluminium in the brains of people with Alzheimer's but other studies have found no link.

In 2006, *The Times* reported the death of a 58-year-old woman from a rare form of Alzheimer's after being exposed to high levels of aluminium for nearly 20 years. But this was aluminium in very high quantities for a very long period of time – when 20 tonnes of aluminium sulphate was dumped into a local water supply.

Cholesterol has also been widely blamed for causing Alzheimer's, resulting in many people taking cholesterol lowering drugs to try and prevent it. Again, no clear link has been determined, with various pieces of research contradicting each other.

It is a well studied area but a conclusive link has yet to be found. At this stage it is probably wise to remember that one of the causes of high cholesterol is poor diet. Diet is one of the stronger links scientists are investigating and it could be this rather than cholesterol which is to blame.

What part do family genes play?

The role of genetics is becoming more prominent, with the first baby having recently been born free of the breast cancer gene. However, we should be very aware of genetics and what we cannot prevent.

To a certain extent, the impact of family genetics on your risk of developing Alzheimer's has been overstated. Many people take it as written in stone that if one of their parents had it, they will develop it. However, like many conditions, it is not that simple.

Only 5% of Alzheimer's cases are diagnosed in those aged 30 to 60 and it is in a certain type of early-onset Alzheimer's called familial AD that the genetic aspect comes in. Inheriting even one of the mutant genes of familial AD from a parent means that the person will have a high chance of developing Alzheimer's.

There is a gene which increases your risk of late-onset Alzheimer's but it must be noted that this is just an increase and is not a certainty. Much research still needs to be conducted into this area – there are several genes involved, some of which we still know little about.

Like many conditions, you can inherit the genes which make you more susceptible to Alzheimer's but this does not necessarily mean you will develop it. This isn't an area which you should spend much time pondering. If one of your parents had Alzheimer's, it is most likely that their illness was caused by a variety of lifestyle and environmental factors. There may well be a slight increase in the chances of you passing the gene on to your children, but energy should be put into what you can change, not what you can't.

Research on causes

As stated earlier, it really is important that research into Alzheimer's is conducted. In fact, considering the amount of people who have Alzheimer's and its growing prevalence in the population, many people feel that not enough money is spent on research.

The amount of research studies and findings can be baffling, with different studies saying different things. So what has it achieved so far and how near are we to finding causes and a cure?

Despite no direct cause being found, researchers have been able to pinpoint some of the factors which increase a person's chance of developing Alzheimer's. People who smoke or have high blood pressure or high cholesterol have an increased risk of developing Alzheimer's. This does not mean that they are acknowledged as direct causes, but it does mean that it is likely that the answer to what is the cause possibly lies at least partly in our lifestyle.

It is also likely that keeping the brain active could help prevent onset. A study conducted in New York in 2003 found that doing a crossword puzzle at least four times a week greatly reduced a person's chance of developing dementia. This has been taken on board by companies such as Nintendo whose Nintendo DS, previously marketed mainly at children, is now also being marketed at older people with the launch of its Brain Age game and with TV adverts showing this age group enjoying the game.

A fit and active brain should also be accompanied by a fit and active body, and several research studies have confirmed a connection between lack of regular exercise and an increased chance in developing Alzheimer's. One Swedish study found that regular exercise can halve a person's chance of developing the disease. Another study published in the *British Medical Journal* found that overweight people were 70% more likely to develop Alzheimer's.

Why is this? Well, a lot is probably down to the fact that exercise increases the blood supply to the brain, keeping it active and prolonging its health. Many of the research findings can be linked to keeping the brain active and healthy, whether through crosswords and other puzzles, healthy food which nourishes the brain (like oily fish) or by ensuring that the brain receives a good blood supply through exercise.

While no direct cause has been found as yet, it is generally accepted that a healthy lifestyle is the best way at present of preventing the disease.

Coming to terms with it

The whole 'why me?' dilemma is very much part of accepting the diagnosis. But how do you come to terms with the fact that you have been diagnosed with a disease that has no cure and which will only get worse over time? It is not easy and everyone has their own way of coping. At first you may decide to fight it and to not change your life, but you will eventually find that this is not possible and may end up making everything more upsetting.

Much has to do with the speed of onset and how early you are diagnosed. The earlier a diagnosis has been made, the more time you will have to make plans and to come to terms with the disease.

Everyone is different. Some people see diagnosis as a relief, knowing that there is a medical reason for why things have been happening to them and that it is not something like a brain tumour or cancer. Others may view it negatively and may go through a period of depression.

The length of time it takes to accept what is happening will vary depending on the individual and their situation. But acceptance can allow you to move on a stage, to plan for the future and to make the necessary changes. It can be the start of accepting help – emotional as well as physical. Acceptance can allow you to start talking positively with support workers, to take steps to join support groups, to make friends with others in the same situation and perhaps to help each other.

However, more often than not, acceptance is harder for the family. Relatives can often take some time to come to terms with the fact that an Alzheimer's diagnosis has been made. This can involve denial or searching for an alternative diagnosis and can often go on for some time. It is not unusual for the relatives of people in the later stages of Alzheimer's to still be in a state of denial.

Summing Up

- Asking 'why me?' is inevitable and it is understandable that you will want to know why and how it has happened to you.

- Due to the nature of the illness, it is harder to pin down the causes of Alzheimer's, with more being known about other forms of dementia.

- Genetics and a family link are often mentioned but it is not as clear cut as this and differences exist between early-onset and late-onset dementia.

- Research is constantly going on into causes and cures. We may not have the answers yet but every research study which is carried out takes us one step closer.

- Looking for a cause and a reason may be the first step in accepting Alzheimer's.

- Initial denial is understandable but acceptance does allow for action to be taken and plans to be made.

- Family often find it harder to come to terms with the situation and this may continue long term.

Chapter Six

Steps to Take

Often diagnosis takes a while and the time following it can seem a bit empty. Many people have spent months, sometimes years, trying to get a diagnosis. Once this has been achieved, it is hard to know what to do next. You may feel that you should be doing something, making changes to your life and preparing for the future but when, and where, do you start?

What you should do

Experts do agree that an earlier diagnosis is better. Steps can be taken to slow progression and drugs can be prescribed to do this. It can also put minds at rest, particularly if there have been worries about the real cause of the symptoms. It allows other conditions to be ruled out and for focus to be put on the true cause.

Where partners or other family members have been at a loss to explain the strange behaviour, diagnosis can bring a new level of understanding.

Only a few decades ago, a diagnosis was only made when the symptoms had got so bad that it really was quite obvious. When the doctor mentioned Alzheimer's, it was more a confirmation of what the family already knew.

Nowadays, people are diagnosed much earlier on and often keep on working and living a normal life. A diagnosis of Alzheimer's did not stop the author Terry Pratchett from writing!

There really isn't any rush to do anything. It is very likely that you will have plenty of time to adjust and to make preparations. Take some time to get used to the idea, to read up on Alzheimer's and to think about what you want and where you feel you need to make changes.

'Experts do agree that an earlier diagnosis is better. Steps can be taken to slow progression and drugs can be prescribed to do this.'

The first thing you may want to do is tell family and friends. They should be able to provide you with support, both emotionally and physically, when required. Friends may have already given you much support as you have gone through tests and visits to specialists. But even if you have decided to do things on your own, at some stage friends and family will need to be told.

Following diagnosis is a good time to speak to your GP or specialist about medication. The early stage of the disease is the time when medication is most effective. It also allows time for medication to be changed should it be required. There are several drugs available – talk to your GP or specialist to find out which one suits you best. Ask about your options and take the time to decide what medication, if any, you would prefer to take.

'The first thing you may want to do is tell family and friends. They should be able to provide you with support, both emotionally and physically, when required.'

If you haven't done so already, you should start thinking about nutrition and what you eat. Weight loss in the middle to later stages of Alzheimer's is a common symptom, so it is advisable to optimise nutrient intake at this stage.

A good, regular diet from the different food groups is recommended. Much research has been conducted into the benefits of different food groups in preventing Alzheimer's, but at this stage the focus should be on preventing any vitamin deficiencies or anaemia, ensuring a healthy all round approach is taken.

Life doesn't end once you have been diagnosed! There is still plenty you can do – by staying active you can help to avoid insomnia which should go some way to helping prevent depression. Don't immediately rule out going to the places you usually go to or holidaying in places you have always dreamt of visiting. In many respects, now is the time to do these things.

As explained earlier, there is much evidence that keeping the mind active is good for slowing down the onset of the disease which is why it is a good idea to take up a new interest. Whether it be art, films, the theatre or visiting museums, if you don't already do so, consider looking into taking up a hobby which will keep your mind active and occupy your time.

Finally, think about the future and what you want. Make plans for when you can no longer drive. Plan ahead and tell those close to you of your wishes. At some stage, you will need to think about who you want to look after your affairs – speak to someone about probate and who you would like to nominate to have power of attorney.

Changes to make to your life

While most of us like our independence and want to hold on to it for as long as possible, there is no shame in asking for help, and it is certainly worth it if this will allow you a better quality of life and enable you to manage on your own for longer.

If you need help with the housework, arrange for this. If family can't help, look into employing a cleaner if possible. Speak to friends and neighbours who may be able to recommend someone.

Consider setting up direct debits for all of your bills. This will save having to go out to pay them and will reduce the number of occasions where you may have problems handling money.

Through time you will find that you will have good days and bad days, as well as times of the day when you are not doing so well. Accept this. Aim to do difficult tasks at a time of day when you tend to feel best. If you are having a bad day, accept this and adjust your schedule. Decide what doesn't need to be done immediately and plan to do it another day when you are feeling more able.

Take your time with tasks which do need to be done and don't let anyone hurry you. Plan your day so that you are not rushed and allow yourself more time than you would have done previously.

Try and arrange activities regularly so that you have a reason for getting up and going out. Keep a bit of routine.

'There is much evidence that keeping the mind active is good for slowing down the onset of the disease, which is why it is a good idea to take up a new interest.'

Changes which may help with the disease

As remembering gets more difficult, there are many things you can do to help trigger your memory. Arrange for a friend or family member to remind you of any appointments you have. If you find that you have started forgetting important telephone numbers, keep a list of the ones you call most regularly beside the telephone for easy access.

Many people find that triggers work. To help you avoid forgetting the date, pick up a small date-per-page calendar where you turn over the page at the start of each day.

A 2009 study conducted at the Mayo Clinic in the USA suggested that activities such as reading, playing games, using a computer and doing craft activities can reduce the risk of memory loss. However, the Nintendo DS, which many elderly people buy and use to stave off dementia, has recently been criticised for being no more effective than using the computer or doing a crossword. So, there is no need to spend a lot of money but, if it takes your fancy, a Nintendo DS is a fun way of passing the time and keeping the brain active.

'A 2009 study conducted at the Mayo Clinic in the USA suggested that activities such as reading, playing games, using a computer and doing craft activities can reduce the risk of memory loss.'

Ensure that you don't begin to become isolated and that you still go out often. Consider visiting a day centre on a regular basis. Investigate what there is available locally and where the nearest day centre is. Most day centres will pick you up and drop you off so you don't need to worry about getting there and back.

Day centres can help by providing a routine and social activities with others in the same position. They will organise stimulating projects, help you with memory exercises and may organise days out to local attractions.

What not to worry about

Worrying can get so bad that you end up worrying about worrying. Don't! Many of your worries will be unfounded and will just make you more stressed.

Don't worry about taking up too much of people's time or about asking for help from friends and family. Most people will be only too pleased to help. The people who care about you will want to help you in any way they can.

Don't worry if some days are worse than others. The chances are that tomorrow will be better. After a while you will get used to the ups and downs, and will learn to adjust your life to suit.

Most of all, remember that worrying will not help – if it goes on too long, it can lead to depression. Speak to people about your concerns and ensure that your mind is put at rest. Don't keep things to yourself – speak to people about any worries you have. The more you think about things, the worse the situation can seem.

Who can help

There are various places you can go for help, but you should first start with your family and friends. While you can access professional help, emotional and practical support from the people who care about you cannot be replaced. Friends and family can be there for you long term. They know you and hopefully at times will offer help without you needing to ask.

Some people will offer help straightaway, but others might not know whether to offer or not in case they offend you. Sometimes you have to make the first move and ask for help. You may find that they have been waiting for you to ask all along.

Organisations to approach

Your local authority is a good place to start in order to access services. In some parts of the country, the department to contact is called Direct Care Services, but it is best to look into this locally. They will tell you what services and help you are due. In some cases they can arrange a cleaner for you, should you require it.

At the end of 2008, the government announced plans for memory clinics in every town. Memory clinics can provide treatment for people with Alzheimer's. They have been around since the late 1980s but have really taken off in the last 10 years.

The website www.memoryclinic.com is a good place to start. As well as providing background information on what memory clinics are and how they can help you, there is a database of clinics in the UK. The Glasgow Memory

'While you can access professional help, emotional and practical support from the people who care about you cannot be replaced.'

Clinic was established in 2000 and is now based within a purpose built facility at the West of Scotland Science Park, Bearsden, Glasgow. Others, such as the South Manchester Memory Clinic, are based within a hospital.

The Alzheimer's Society and Alzheimer's Scotland can also provide support and advice, and are excellent points of reference for the times when you don't know who to turn to and don't know what services you can access. They can also put you in touch with other organisations that can help.

In various parts of the country there are dementia helplines available, some offering a 24-hour service. These can provide the support needed when all you need is someone to talk to. Both the Alzheimer's Society and Alzheimer's Scotland run dementia helplines, as do organisations such as For Dementia, whose helpline is manned by Admiral Nurses.

Summing Up

- There is no immediate rush to take action but you should spend time considering what you want for the future.

- The first people you should tell are friends and family.

- Keep active mentally and physically. Keep up an interest in life and living.

- Making small changes will result in life being easier for you.

- Don't be afraid to ask for help.

- Worrying will not help and will only upset you. Speak to people about any concerns you have.

- Friends and family should be able to help but there are organisations you can also turn to.

- The Alzheimer's Society and Alzheimer's Scotland are two of the best places to start.

'Worrying will not help and will only upset you. Speak to people about any concerns you have.'

Chapter Seven

Friends and Family

Friends and family may have been there for you from the start. Or perhaps, for various reasons, they may not know about the problems you have been having. A friend or family member may have been with you when you received a diagnosis. If so, this person could help you decide how to tell people and what to tell them.

When to tell friends and family

There is no easy answer to this. In an ideal situation, those closest to you will already know that you have been going for tests and the subject may have come up when discussing what could be wrong. They may have given you much support already and may have helped you prepare for such an outcome. Sometimes family and friends are the ones to notice changes first, or to at least voice their concerns.

This all depends on the strength of the relationship and how close you are. Sometimes it is the people closest to us who are the hardest to tell and they can take the news badly. These are the people who are likely to feel it most and who could have stronger feelings. These are the people who will be around as your condition progresses and to whom the term 'Alzheimer's' will have more meaning.

You may find that you need some time to yourself to get used to the news before you begin telling anyone else. Even if you have had your suspicions, it may well still come as a shock and it may take you a bit of time to accept.

Many people feel that they are in a better position to explain to other people once they have had some time to themselves to adjust. It allows you to get used to the idea and to prepare for other people's reactions and questions.

But don't spend too much time pondering on this issue. People can be surprising – you may find that once you start telling people, life becomes easier as you start being offered more support.

The decision of when to tell people is ultimately yours. If those close to you already know, it could be an idea for them to tell others for you.

Remember how you felt when you were first given the diagnosis. Think about the mixture of emotions you felt. Be prepared for the fact that you may be hit by a variety of reactions when you tell people. But people's initial reactions may be just that and they may react quite differently once the news has sunk in.

What to tell them and how

'You may find that once you start telling people, life becomes easier as you start being offered more support.'

You may think this is obvious. 'I have Alzheimer's' does cover all bases and to a certain extent it is best to get straight to the point. However, the news is likely to prompt lots of discussion, either straightaway or when the realisation of the news sets in.

Choose a time when people are not too busy. Telling anyone news when they are preoccupied is not likely to result in the best reaction and could mean you go away with the incorrect impression that the person does not care. Ensure that the person you are telling has time to listen.

While we have come a long way since the old fashioned, incorrect ideas and opinions of yesteryear, some of these still linger. Don't be too surprised if people ask what you think are stupid questions. Be patient and remember that people do sometimes say silly things without thinking – things they really don't mean. Others may simply be keen to find out more and may unfortunately be voicing their opinions in the wrong way.

Often it is easier to tell some people by telephone, allowing them time to get used to the idea. They may want to ask you questions at a later date – remember that you have probably had a bit of time to get used to the idea, so others will need this too.

Once the news has sunk in, be prepared for lots of questions and for them to snowball once a few have been asked. Many people have little knowledge of the disease and will feel that they owe it to you to find out more. You probably won't be able to answer all their questions but you can point them in the direction of sources of information.

After telling the first few people, you may find that things get easier and that you have the answers ready. But people can still surprise you.

Telling young children

Children can be very accepting of people's behaviour and in many cases you will not need to tell them. If you are regularly making mistakes, it is likely that children will notice and comment on it. But in most cases children laugh at these things, thinking their grandparent is just being silly or pretending.

Whether you tell the children in your family or not depends very much on their age and maturity level. If you do not, the children's parents may tell them. They will hopefully consider both you and the children and decide what they need to know.

The children's parents should judge each situation as it arises. Older people do gain a lot from the company of young children and it is a good idea to encourage such relationships. But at the same time, if the person with Alzheimer's begins to get aggressive or shows signs of unacceptable behaviour, they should remove the child.

Who to tell outside the family

Who should you tell other than family and friends? Do you really need to tell other people?

This really isn't a priority and is nothing to spend time worrying about. Only tell who you want to and who you feel needs to know. If you are on friendly terms with the neighbours, tell them. It will allow them to look out for you should you need help or have an accident. A neighbour may offer to start looking in on you or to do shopping for you.

'Children can be very accepting of people's behaviour and in many cases you will not need to tell them.'

If you regularly attend church, you may find comfort confiding in people there. You may also want to tell people who you see regularly – acquaintances rather than friends.

Coping with other people's reactions

It is likely that you will be met with a variety of reactions as everyone acts differently to such news. Some might be supportive and offer you emotional and practical support. They might provide an extra ear to listen when you are upset or have concerns.

Others might be dismissive, not believing that Alzheimer's exists, or feel that you don't show what they believe to be the symptoms of the disease. Their picture of people with Alzheimer's may be of someone further down the line and they may not categorise your symptoms as being those of someone with Alzheimer's. They may question the doctor's diagnosis and may tell you that they think the specialist is wrong.

Others might display no reaction whatsoever, showing no signs that they have really taken in what you have said and making no effort to show any support.

It is great to receive immediate support from loved ones, but don't be too disheartened if some people don't react the way you expect. It often takes time.

Coping with negative reactions

Being met with negative reactions can be very upsetting. At a time when you need family and friends the most, it can feel that they have let you down. Coming to terms with Alzheimer's can be hard enough, but having to cope with other people's reactions can seem like a step too far. It may be useful to understand why people react the way they do.

First of all are the people who don't believe you. Lack of knowledge may mean that they simply don't know enough about the disease and may base their opinions around the limited portrayals they have seen in the media.

Time may change their mind – but it may not. There probably isn't much you can do about this and you shouldn't stress yourself in doing so. Increasing media coverage of Alzheimer's may hit them eventually or someone else with a sharp tongue may force them to alter their opinions.

If the person reacting badly is near your own age, he or she may have their own personal reasons for reacting in such a way. The realisation may have hit them that it could very well be them with Alzheimer's and it could be their life changing forever. Some people find it difficult to cope with such things and may not have the strength of character to react well. The best thing you can do is accept this. You can't change people's personalities and shouldn't try.

Others may be upset for you and may not know how to react and what support to offer. They might not know what to say or do and could say something inappropriate when they do try. Realise that sometimes people do say things they don't mean without thinking, things they are likely to regret later.

There are also the people with unrealistic expectations of miracle cures. They care about you and it is their way of keeping positive and doing something for you.

Always remember that the initial reactions you are met with may just be temporary. Think how long it has taken you to get used to having Alzheimer's. Even before diagnosis you would have had time to get used to the idea. Friends and family need that time too. The person who called you a liar or who simply showed no reaction at all may be the one who, a year down the line, is phoning you up to offer help or who admits to you that they have had their eyes opened.

Case study

'I had a mixed reaction from friends and family. Some weren't interested and others did not believe the diagnosis. I think some didn't want to believe it because they just couldn't cope. But a small group of friends were understanding and continue to be so. They ask how I am getting on and offer me assistance. Others have taken time to get used to the idea and are now more supportive, especially my brother.' Sadie, aged 75.

'If the person reacting badly is near your own age, he or she may have their own personal reasons for reacting in such a way. The realisation may have hit them very suddenly that life does not go on the same forever, that it could very well be them with Alzheimer's.'

Summing Up

- It can be hard to tell the people closest to you that you have been diagnosed with Alzheimer's.

- You may find that you need time to get used to the idea yourself before you tell others, or you may feel that they can provide the support you need at this time.

- Choose your time carefully and don't announce it when someone is preoccupied with other things.

- Be prepared for lots of questions. If you can't answer them, point friends and family in the direction of good sources of information.

- Reactions are likely to be mixed and some people might act quite negatively towards the diagnosis.

- Negative reactions can be due to a number of factors and should not upset you.

- It takes some people time to get used to the idea and you may find that the people who react badly just need time to accept it.

'Be prepared for lots of questions. If you can't answer them, point friends and family in the direction of good sources of information.'

Chapter Eight

What Do You Need to Plan For?

Telling those close to you will be your priority. Once you have told family and friends, they can assist you in planning for the future and informing the relevant authorities. There are people you are legally obliged to tell such as the Driver and Vehicle Licensing Agency (DVLA) and insurance companies, but there are also legal steps you should take in order to make life easier later on. When you feel you are up to it, you should sit down with someone close to you and discuss what needs to be done.

Power of attorney

While you are able to, it is best to plan for the future and ensure that you make the decision about who will look after your affairs when it all gets too much. This will take pressure off you and your family but will also mean that you can relay your preferences now and ensure that the person you have nominated takes your wishes into account.

England and Wales

Lasting power of attorney (LPA) replaced enduring power of attorney on 1 October 2007. A power of attorney is a legal document which allows you to nominate a person to look after your affairs on your behalf. You don't have to consult a solicitor but it is certainly a good idea.

'While you are able to, it is best to plan for the future and ensure that you make the decision about who will look after your affairs when it all gets too much. This will take pressure off you and your family.'

Ideally you should choose more than one person to avoid anyone abusing their power and they should be people who will work together. You should consider how well they look after their own finances and affairs and whether they will have your best interests at heart.

There are two types of lasting power of attorney in England and Wales: a property and affairs LPA and a personal welfare LPA. A property and affairs LPA appoints someone to look after your money, property and any other affairs. A personal welfare LPA will make decisions on your health, any treatment you may be offered and on your welfare, for example where you live. Obviously, their decisions will be based on the advice of doctors, nurses, etc.

Before it can be used, the form must be registered at the Office of the Public Guardian. A fee does apply for this.

Scotland

In Scotland there are also two types of power of attorneys – continuing (financial) power of attorney and a welfare power of attorney. A continuing power of attorney appoints someone to look after your money and property, while a welfare power of attorney appoints someone to decide about your personal matters – the medical and care decisions.

One power of attorney can be made to cover both aspects or two separate ones appointing different people. A replacement attorney can also be appointed in case your first choice has to step down.

As in England, the form must be registered at the Office of the Public Guardian (Scotland). A certificate of capacity must accompany the form and should be signed by a solicitor.

Informing the DVLA

If you have been diagnosed with dementia, you are legally obliged to tell the DVLA. By not doing so, you risk a fine of up to £1,000 and your car insurance may become valid.

This does not necessarily mean that you will have to stop driving. If you are still in the early stages of the disease, it may still be possible to carry on driving for some time, but the DVLA will first make an assessment. They will send you a questionnaire and will request a report from your GP.

If you are a carer or relative of someone with Alzheimer's and they refuse to inform the DVLA, you can call the Authority for support. They will then send out what looks like a standard form for the person to fill in which will ask if there is anything they wish to inform the DVLA about, such as dementia.

Speaking to your insurance companies

As just discussed, your motor insurance company should be told as soon as possible. If you don't inform them, you could be breaking the clauses of your agreement which could invalidate your insurance.

People are often caught out because they fail to inform insurance companies of changes to their health or circumstances. So if in doubt, give them a call.

You should also highlight your Alzheimer's when filling out forms for new insurance policies. Some medical and travel insurance policies will not accept applications if the applicant has a pre-existing medical condition, but there are others who will, so it is just a case of shopping around.

Travelling with Alzheimer's

A diagnosis of Alzheimer's should not stop you travelling and going away on holiday. You will be able to judge for yourself what you feel able to do and how far you are able to go. If you have any concerns, speak to the airline or travel company to see if they can assist you in any way.

'People are often caught out because they fail to inform insurance companies of changes to their health or circumstances. So if in doubt, give them a call.'

What adaptations you should consider

Some of the adaptations you should consider will not be necessary but will simply make life easier and help you avoid upset. If you have always been an independent person, asking for help can seem like giving up your independence or giving in to the condition.

But you shouldn't view it like that. You should view it as taking steps to prolong your independence. With additional support you will be able to do a lot more on your own.

The first thing you should look at is your attitude to assistance. The vast majority of people do not mind being asked for help, whether this is asking where the bus stop is because you can't recall its location or asking a stranger how to use a public telephone. It is highly unlikely that they will analyse why you are asking them for help. Most people are too busy. They will assist, accept your thanks and move on, quickly forgetting.

If you don't already, you should arrange for your bills to be paid by direct debit. This will help you avoid forgetting to pay them on time and it means you don't have to worry about going out to pay them or handling money. Paying by direct debit is becoming increasingly common and in many cases results in a discount.

Consider employing a cleaner. If you enjoy housework then great, many people do. But if you feel things are getting on top of you, or if there are some jobs you just aren't able to do, then look around for help. Friends or family may be able to recommend a cleaner or you can contact your local authority. They should be able to arrange for someone to visit regularly.

If you are considering moving nearer your family, now could be a good time to do this. Ask someone to help you look for somewhere and to organise everything with you. Take a long term view of properties and find somewhere you will be happy living in for a long time. Aim to move in plenty of time to settle into a place, rather than moving to new surroundings and meeting new people when you feel less capable.

Looking for local support

With the increasing awareness of dementia, help and support is also increasing. In most areas you will be able to find support, whether that is people to speak to, professional advice or practical support locally. The back of this book includes a list of organisations who can help you or, if not, put you in touch with someone who can.

Once you start looking, you will be surprised at how much help there is out there. But unfortunately this support is not the same throughout the country, with some areas being much better catered for than others. A postcode lottery still exists with regards to dementia services.

Often it is through accessing one means of support that you find out about others. Friends you may make at a support group for people with Alzheimer's may be able to tell you what there is locally which can result in you discovering other services that your local authority provides.

You may also want to look into financial support and investigate what benefits you are due. Even if you feel that you manage fine as you are, you may find that the extra money could pay for services to make life easier for you, such as a cleaner.

Not all benefits are restricted to people on low incomes and some are not means tested. Disability Living Allowance is available for people under the age of 65, with Attendance Allowance being the equivalent for people over 65.

Carers may be able to claim Carer's Allowance if they care for someone for more than 35 hours a week. It is certainly worth investigating what you are due.

'Once you start looking, you will be surprised at how much help there is out there. But unfortunately this support is not the same throughout the country, with some areas being much better catered for than others.'

Preparing for worsening of the disease

At some stage your condition will worsen and this is something you should begin to prepare for now. Organising power of attorney is one of the main steps you should take and it is certainly advisable to have everything in place long before it is needed. Making preparations while you are capable will be much less stressful – it will also allow you time to think properly about things and to not be rushed into making any snap decisions.

It will allow you time to look into care arrangements and to decide about nursing homes. Most nursing homes are used to showing relatives around and would be happy to accommodate you should you wish to visit a few.

But if the idea of choosing a care home upsets you, speak to those close to you and let them know your preferences. Discuss what you do and don't want and ask them to take this into account if you are not able to when the time comes.

Take time to make an action plan, noting what you want to happen and any considerations that you want taken into account. Discuss your plans with those close to you and in particular with the person (or persons) you have appointed as having power of attorney. You should view it as your way of ensuring your wishes are followed.

'Take time to make an action plan, noting what you want to happen and any considerations that you want taken into account.'

Finally, ensure that you leave your affairs in the best order you can. If you haven't already done so, make a will. This will save much time and expense from dying intestate and will make life easier for your family. If you want to put investments into trust, do it now.

Many aspects of planning for the future can be upsetting and it is understandable that some people would prefer to avoid thinking about things, never mind writing their wishes down. However, for some people it can be a relief and something proactive to do.

Nursing homes do admit that although they regularly show people around, in the vast majority of cases these people are relatives and carers and most people prefer not to think too much about reaching this stage.

But dealing with other areas might be reassuring for you. Appointing a power of attorney and settling personal affairs can leave you with a sense of relief that things have been taken care of and that decisions are now in the hands of someone trustworthy.

Summing Up

- As well as family and friends, there are people you are legally obliged to tell about your condition. There are also steps you can follow to take the pressure off you.

- Appointing people with power of attorney should be done early on. A solicitor is not required in England and Wales but you may find that it is worth paying the money for one in order to receive some expert advice.

- While you may still be allowed to drive, legally you do have to inform the DVLA of your diagnosis.

- Make a list of insurance companies you need to inform – motor insurance should be top of that list.

- Don't be afraid to ask for help. Most people are only too happy to assist.

- Look at what local support there is. While this varies throughout the country, through speaking to people in similar circumstances you will find out what is available.

- Make an emergency action plan and let those close to you know what your wishes for the future are.

Chapter Nine

Living with Someone Suffering from Alzheimer's

It is often the people close to you who will first notice the changes which indicate you have Alzheimer's. This chapter is addressed to them – to the husband, wife, son, daughter or sibling. In particular, it is addressed to the spouse or partner who is coping with the person diagnosed with Alzheimer's, living with the condition but feeling its effects in a different way.

Initial reactions

How do you react when you're told that someone you love has been diagnosed with Alzheimer's? How are you supposed to act? What thoughts go through your head?

When someone develops Alzheimer's, they can slowly become a different person. If this person is your spouse, they can appear to no longer be the person you married. We all married for particular reasons and were attracted to our partner for their characteristics. Suddenly it can seem as if that person is no longer there and has been replaced by someone who slowly takes on child-like qualities.

Sadly, marriages can sometimes deteriorate long before the diagnosis as partners struggle to understand why their loved one is acting so out of character. They may put it down to a number of factors such as stress at work or depression, or they may be at a loss for an explanation. Many people state that life would have been easier if a diagnosis had been made earlier.

A diagnosis provides an explanation and a starting point for learning how to cope, but it can also bring a range of emotions including fear. Where once there was fear of the unknown, there is now fear of the known and of the future.

You may feel angry that this has happened to someone you love, sadness at what you have lost or guilt at your lack of patience and anger when things are really bad. If you have had to give up work or cut back on other commitments and activities, you may feel resentment at what you have lost.

Total exhaustion is also inevitable. The work and care can be tiring both mentally and physically. At times you may feel that the stress is getting too much and that you are at the end of your tether.

The dynamics of the relationship may have moved on from being cared for to caring for and you may no longer feel close. But it is important to realise that this is not the end of the relationship – instead, a new one has been formed.

The emotions won't all be negative. There will still be laughter and love, and having a good sense of humour can mean that you both see the funny side of things at times.

Supporting your partner

More than any drugs, doctors or miracle cures, your partner will need you and your support. For some people, this responsibility can seem overwhelming and too much to cope with.

The most important way you can support your partner is by just being there and showing you care. It is necessary to accept the situation and to start taking practical steps in dealing with the condition. Acceptance is vital for everyone.

Aim to gather as much information as possible. There will be people you can turn to who can answer your questions, but when it is late at night and you are sitting alone thinking about things, a book can seem like a friend and can answer so many of your questions before you even ask them.

If you gather as much information as you can, it really will help you discover why Alzheimer's sufferers act the way they do and why they do things so out of character. This really will make it easier to cope. The frustration may still be there but, for example, if you realise that your partner no longer eats cauliflower or potato because their brain does not differentiate it against the white plate, it is easier not to get angry. It also means you know to use coloured plates.

You should not view their decline as losing the person you love but as gaining another side to them. Psychiatric nurses who care for the same people for years are adamant that the person they have got to know in the later stages is still very much a person with their own personality. That person may be very different from the person they were for most of their life but it is definitely still them.

Some couples find that organising some special time together works for them. This can involve a version of a memory book – an album containing photographs from different parts of your life together and press cuttings from major events throughout your life.

Try and bring as much positive into your lives as possible. Life can still be fun – even when it's not, it can help to forget about tomorrow and just concentrate on today.

What to watch out for

Dementia increases the risk of accidents in the home and it is advisable to take steps sooner rather than later to reduce risks. If repairs are required, you should deal with them as soon as possible.

Dangerous liquids such as bleach or paint should be kept safely away. Even if you don't view this as being a problem, you should try to be prepared and take a long term view. An occupational therapist will be able to advise you on things to look out for, changes to make and whether you are able to receive funding to make alterations to your home.

'If you realise that your partner no longer eats cauliflower or potato because their brain does not differentiate it against the white plate, it is easier not to get angry. It also means you know to use coloured plates.'

You should also be aware of changes in the behaviour of your partner and on the look out for signs that the Alzheimer's is progressing. Look for changes in their sleeping pattern, like more afternoon naps, and a lack of orientation with regards to what time of day it is. They may start to forget how to do household tasks such as turning on the washing machine or find they are unable to use the telephone.

A loss of short term memory is one of the best known Alzheimer's symptoms, but you should also look for signs that long term memory is deteriorating. This is more of a problem than something like forgetting to go to the dentist.

If you feel that your partner has started to forget where things are, then steps can easily be taken to help them, like labelling each cupboard in the kitchen.

Wandering can be the most worrying of symptoms. Many people with Alzheimer's take to wandering but are unable to find their way back. If your partner has started to forget how to get back home, it is time to take steps to prevent this. There are tracking devices available marketed at people with dementia as well as various forms of alarm systems which alert the carer that the person with dementia has opened the door to go out. Even a simple set of windchimes at the front door can do the trick.

Support groups for family

Often we can become so engrossed in looking after our partner that we forget to look after ourselves. Eventually this can begin to show itself in our health and behaviour.

Finding time for yourself is not something you should just consider – it is something you must do for yourself and your family. If you have had a bit of a rest and a break from the stress and the focus of caring for someone, you will be much better placed to care for your partner.

It is easy to let hobbies slide and give up on the activities you used to look forward to so much. Many hobbies only take us away from home for a couple of hours at a time, but those couple of hours can give us as much benefit as a holiday.

'A loss of short term memory is one of the best known Alzheimer's symptoms, but you should also look for signs that long term memory is deteriorating. This is more of a problem than something like forgetting to go to the dentist.'

Aim to keep or regain some 'me time' every week. It doesn't have to be anything big or fancy – it could be going for a swim or simply going for a coffee with a friend. It is important to remember that you are a person in your own right and have a separate identity to being a full time carer.

If someone calls round unexpectedly and offers to stay with your partner for an hour or two while you get time for yourself, then don't refuse them.

For many, relief comes in the form of talking and sharing problems and experiences. There is nobody better placed for listening and understanding than those who have been through, or who are going through, the same thing.

Friends may give you advice, and it is good to talk to people you know and trust, but support groups provide that added extra because most people there have or have had a similar experience to you. They can provide you with the words of wisdom as only someone in the know can.

Try to organise a visit to a support group and see if it suits you. Having a set event to go to each week means that it is harder for you to change your mind at the last moment. View it as part of your weekly routine and ensure that if you have to organise for someone to be there with your partner that they understand how important it is for you.

When things get worse

There are no timescales for when your partner's condition will progress. It could be months, it could be years, but while there is no point focusing on what has still to come, it is best to be prepared.

Discuss with your loved one what they want to happen and how they want to be cared for in the later stages. Make all the decisions long in advance when your partner is still well enough to do so. If you feel that it would be easier, and would cause fewer problems particularly with other family members, write down these wishes and keep them safe. If you have children, sit down together with them, long before you need to, and tell them what your partner's wishes are.

The worsening of the condition will be a gradual process and will not happen overnight. Don't ignore it – take the time to put plans into motion. It is likely that you have slowly begun to make changes both in the house and in your lifestyle.

When the time comes, respect your partner's wishes. Try and take a step back when making decisions. You may want to keep caring for your partner at home, but there might come a time when you will need help. Go and look at nursing homes and look at the extras they offer and the added company they can provide. Take advice from different people about the best thing to do.

Most of all, get rid of any guilt you have. Guilt is a very, very common emotion in relatives who have a loved one in the later stages of dementia. Just do what you can and be there for them. Guilt is a negative emotion which will just eat away at you and will do neither of you any good.

'Don't start feeling guilty. It is a negative emotion which will just eat away at you and will do neither of you any good.'

Summing Up

- Marriages often deteriorate long before the diagnosis of Alzheimer's as couples struggle to deal with the change in one partner's personality. Knowing what is actually wrong can be a relief.

- It can seem as if you have lost the person you love. You should not focus on the aspects of the person you have lost but on what you have now. There can still be fun and laughter.

- Gather as much information as possible about Alzheimer's, why certain things happen and why sufferers do things a certain way. It will help you understand and reduce frustration.

- Be aware of the signs that the disease is worsening and be prepared for them.

- Take time for yourself on a regular basis. Find a carers' support group you feel comfortable with and continue with any hobbies or interests you have.

- The time will come when the condition worsens. While you should focus on the present day, you should not ignore the inevitable. Be prepared and talk about it together. Know what your partner wants.

Chapter Ten

When a Parent is Diagnosed

When a parent is diagnosed with Alzheimer's, it can send shockwaves through the family. Some of the family may be a bit more removed from the situation, so the diagnosis can come as a shock. There may be a period of denial, with some relatives not agreeing with the diagnosis and pushing for a second opinion.

If you are the one doing most of the caring, it may start to feel as if you have swapped roles and that you have become the parent. You may begin to resent this reversal of roles or find that you fall into the role far too easily, causing friction as your parent resents you for treating them like a child.

Trying to maintain your own life can be hard as the responsibilities increase. If you have always been an independent person, having to consider someone else all the time can be difficult.

Friction within families is very common in the later stages. If you are an only child, it can seem unfair that you are left to deal with everything and you may wish that you had a sibling to share the responsibility. But even in larger families, the idealistic situation of all siblings pulling together and taking turns does not always happen. Often one person takes on most of the care. Siblings may live too far away to take much of an active role, they may have young children or a job which takes up much of their time or they might simply be quite happy for one person to deal with everything. This can cause no end of resentment and bad feeling in families, often leading to relationship breakdowns.

It may help to try and resolve this issue before it really begins. If one sibling takes complete control right from the start, others can begin to accept this as the norm. Perhaps it does suit that person to be in charge at that point, but this is likely to not always be the case. As more care is needed and it becomes harder for one person to cope, that person may begin to look to their family for more assistance. By that time the rest of the family have accepted the set up.

A more sensible course of action is to try and share the load right from the very start. Get brothers and sisters involved in decision making and helping out. Ensure that they understand the work and responsibility involved and that it should really be shared.

How to support your parent

'Children, in particular grandchildren, bring a lot of pleasure to the elderly, and people with Alzheimer's are no different. Children can be a really positive escape from the mundane and can be particularly good for those with depression.'

Children, in particular grandchildren, bring a lot of pleasure to the elderly, and people with Alzheimer's are no different. Children can be a really positive escape from the mundane and can be particularly good for those with depression. It can be a real boost to see someone's face light up when a child walks into the room.

Grandchildren can be good for reality orientation. They act as a trigger for the Alzheimer's sufferer to remember who they are and where they fit into the family. In an indirect way, you can get them to think about this, discussing who the child is and other details.

The grandparent may well forget the child's name but children are amazingly adaptable and may well find it funny. It really is a case of judging every situation as it arises.

Frequency and length of visits will be dependent on many factors, including the age and activity level of the child as well as what the person with Alzheimer's can cope with. Boisterous children may soon get too much and the noise level may irritate. This is easy enough to judge and should not be ignored.

However, you should not ignore the needs of the child either. For visits to go well, the child must enjoy visiting and not get bored. If the person with Alzheimer's is incontinent, it may be a good idea to try and avoid staying to the point where the child notices and comments on the fact.

Another positive activity which involves all the family is to make up a life story book. A life story book is a personal account of all things and people which are important in that person's life. For someone with Alzheimer's, this can act as a fun prompt, where someone can sit down with them and go through who is in each picture. Each picture acts as a reason to talk about that person or place and topics leading off from that. It triggers the brain to think about things.

A life story book can also be a good keepsake for younger members of the family at a time when the family is losing that link with the past. You can buy ready made life story books designed for you to insert pictures or you can use a scrap book and make your own.

Ways you can help – questions

What is the right and wrong thing to do when someone has Alzheimer's? Families are often at a loss over whether to go along with what the person thinks or to correct them. In this section we go over some commonly asked questions from relatives.

Question: should I correct my mother if she gets me confused with my sister?

Answer: this really depends if this is a trigger point or not. Will it benefit your mother to know the difference? Will it help her remember other things related to you or your sister? If the answer is yes and it doesn't upset her, then it would be a good idea to correct her.

However, don't do this if it upsets her. Upsetting her will not help her to remember and will do no good whatsoever.

Question: my mother refers to my dad as if he is still alive. Should I tell her the truth or go along with pretending?

Answer: sometimes you have to tell little white lies in order to protect the person with Alzheimer's. As with the above, think about whether the news will upset her or not. If your mum is going to react as if she is hearing the news for the first time and is going to get upset and grieve for your dad, then it is not a good idea to put her through that. The best thing to do is to side step the issue and avoid telling her either the truth or lies.

Question: my wife has had a few falls and I am worried she is really going to hurt herself next time. I try to keep the house obstacle free but don't know what else to do.

Answer: an occupational therapist will be able to advise you on this and will come out to your home to conduct an assessment. But there are a couple of pointers to consider. Ensure that each room is adequately lit, that the light bulbs are bright enough and that there are no dark corners.

Don't forget to look at what carpets are in the house. There has been much research conducted into how the mind works when someone develops dementia. One of the things that has been discovered is that swirly or patterned carpets can disorientate someone with Alzheimer's.

One of the most common causes of falls is badly fitting footwear. If a person is wearing the wrong sized shoes, it increases their chances of tripping up. They may also be wearing unsuitable footwear, for example they could have shoes which require the laces to be tied but they forget to do so.

'One of the things that has been discovered is that swirly or patterned carpets can draw a person into the pattern and can disorientate them.'

Question: my uncle is now at the point where he can't manage on his own but none of the family can take him in. He refuses to go into a home. What can we do?

Answer: your uncle has to realise that a nursing home is probably the best place for him but at the same time you can't force him. Keep trying to talk him round and try to convince him that it is in his best interests. If you feel that you are getting nowhere, try getting someone else to speak to him – a social worker or CPN perhaps.

Things to take into account

As the person with Alzheimer's begins to deteriorate, they may become anxious and upset at their situation. In the early stages, they may want to talk about their concerns. It is important that you take the time to sit down and listen rather than dismissing their concerns. Show them you are there for them and support them in expressing their feelings.

Always make them feel valued and give them the respect they are due. Don't let Alzheimer's become too much of a label. Remember they are a person in their own right and not simply someone who suffers from Alzheimer's.

As the disease progresses, it is all too easy to start thinking of the person differently. Try to respect their privacy and if the person is incontinent, aim to deal with this in a sensitive manner.

Avoid speaking to the person as if they are a child and, whenever possible, speak with them, not about them. Try not to stand in front of them and discuss them with another person as if they aren't there.

Caring for someone with Alzheimer's is more than just about caring for their physical needs. Aim to read as much about the disease as possible and try to understand why they do certain things and act a certain way.

Case study

'Mum had never liked her brother's wife but things stayed cool and cordial until the last few years when he started to develop Alzheimer's. Mum would not accept it or recognise that that was what he had. My uncle lived abroad and got to the stage where he could not write or visit. Mum decided that it was a conspiracy by his family to keep them apart.

'I tried speaking to her directly about it but she would just get incredibly angry with me, and it ended up affecting our relationship. He is dead now and she still doesn't accept that he had Alzheimer's.' Michael, aged 52.

'Don't let Alzheimer's become too much of a label. Remember they are a person in their own right and not simply someone who suffers from Alzheimer's.'

Summing Up

■ Alzheimer's can send shockwaves through the family and can be the cause of a lot of family friction.

■ Often, one person ends up doing most of the caring. This can lead to resentment between siblings.

■ Caring for a parent can be hard and the set up can slowly change to one where you feel that roles have been reversed, with you taking on the position of parent.

■ From the start, try to ensure that one person is not left to do everything.

■ Grandchildren can be very therapeutic for people with Alzheimer's. What you tell the child and how you organise visits depends very much on the situation and the child.

■ Consider making a life story book – both to aid the person's memory and as a lasting reminder for the whole family.

■ Always aim to give the person respect and to avoid treating and speaking to them as if they are a child.

Chapter Eleven

The Future

While in some ways it is best to take every day as it comes, you can't help worrying about the future. However, planning what you want can help put your mind at rest. Ideally, you will have dealt with your affairs, leaving you free of this worry as the disease progresses.

Is it all bleak?

Alzheimer's forces you and your family to reassess life and what the future holds. Care staff often get asked by family members how long the person has. In 99% of cases, they simply can't answer that. Alzheimer's has no life plan and nobody can tell you when things will progress or how long you have before you reach the final stages.

To a certain extent, you can't plan for the future in detail and should focus on the present. But there are plans you can put into place which require no time scales. As previously mentioned, dealing with your financial affairs can be a load off your mind.

People who have been diagnosed with Alzheimer's often worry about what will happen when they become too ill to look after themselves. A social worker or CPN will be able to discuss this with you and can tell you what services are available in your area.

The Alzheimer's Society encourages people to put together an advanced statement. In England and Wales, the Mental Capacity Act 2005 gave people a statutory right to refuse treatment via the use of an advanced statement. An advanced statement allows a person to state what treatment they do and do not want should they reach the stage where they are unable to decide for themselves.

'There are plans you can put into place which require no time scales. As previously mentioned, dealing with your financial affairs can be a load off your mind.'

As long as the statement is valid and applicable, it is legally enforceable in England and Wales. However, it cannot be used to refuse basic nursing care or to ask for anything which is against the law such as euthanasia.

An advanced statement should state what sort of treatment you would prefer and your views on life-prolonging treatments. You should discuss it with your GP to ensure that what you write is valid and not conflicting, and also with close family members so they are fully aware of what it contains.

It is best to leave a copy with your lawyer and a close relative, and to review it regularly in case you wish to make any changes. The Alzheimer's Society can provide you with a form which outlines what it should contain.

'According to figures from the Alzheimer's Research Trust, £11 per head is spent each year in the UK on research for a cure, compared with £289 for each cancer patient.'

What is being done to look for a cure?

In many ways we have come a long way since Alois Alzheimer discovered the disease 100 years ago. But in many ways it may seem as if we have not. Large steps have been taken in the last 20-30 years but much work is still needed.

The words 'Alzheimer's cure' hit the headlines regularly and millions of people read on hoping that it will say that a cure has definitely been found and that the destruction it causes can now be reversed. Still, time rolls on with no such news but the hope does continue.

According to figures from the Alzheimer's Research Trust, £11 per head is spent each year in the UK on research for a cure, compared with £289 for each cancer patient. This is despite similar numbers of people being affected.

In November 2008, best-selling author Terry Pratchett met with the prime minister Gordon Brown to hand him a petition containing 18,000 signatures demanding more cash for research into Alzheimer's disease. Pratchett's diagnosis of Alzheimer's has helped keep the disease in the headlines. He is doing his utmost to lobby for more money to be used to find a cure and has donated millions of his own to the cause.

This does not mean that little is being done to achieve this aim. Research is continuing all the time and some scientists are becoming increasingly confident that a cure will be found in the next five years.

There have been many trials with positive results, too many to name here, but still nothing concrete. However, despite the low level of funding, there is work going on. An optimistic way of looking at things is that with each research trial, more is discovered about the disease and how it works. The Alzheimer's Research Trust describe it as parts of a jigsaw, with each piece contributing to the final completion of the puzzle.

Other research being conducted

Research is paramount to both a cure and a cause being found. To help understand the disease we need to know as much as possible about its causes, why certain changes happen and what exactly happens to the brain.

The Alzheimer's Research Trust has funded over 150 research projects looking at ways to prevent, cure or treat dementia. One research project it has funded has found a DNA link to Lewy body disease and Parkinson's disease, helping scientists to identify routes to potential treatments. A second project identified markers in the blood for the development of Alzheimer's for the first time, offering hope of a possible blood test to diagnose the disease. And a third project screened 1.5 million compounds, identifying 40 which offer the greatest potential to be developed into drugs for treating Alzheimer's.

'The Alzheimer's Research Trust has funded over 150 research projects looking at ways to prevent, cure or treat dementia.'

Currently, the Trust is funding work at the universities of Manchester and Newcastle. This work is building on a pilot study which suggested that aromatherapy may have a beneficial effect on agitation. It also involves studying the effects a new group of compounds could have on slowing down or halting dementia, plus investigations into the brain changes of people with Alzheimer's.

The Alzheimer's Research Trust links 15 research centres throughout the UK. Among many studies into the disease, it is currently funding research into a link between diabetes and Alzheimer's, a study into predicting responses to cholinesterase inhibitors, and the role of stress in the biochemistry of Alzheimer's.

Other universities and research institutes throughout the country are conducting research into the area and work is ongoing. With an ageing population, Alzheimer's is going to affect more people, so there will be an even greater need for a cure. Nobody knows how close to finding a cure we are, but learning more about the causes and progression must surely help build up a clearer picture of the disease.

Case studies

Heather, aged 54

'My mum is nearly 83 and was diagnosed with Alzheimer's two years ago. She is still capable in many respects – she can wash and feed herself and isn't incontinent. She still has her own house but I don't let her sleep there. She eats and sleeps at mine and goes down to her own place during the day. It is only five minutes down the road and I do think she enjoys the freedom.

'Caring for someone with Alzheimer's has affected my freedom to a certain extent. I can't just go away and leave her on her own but I can still go out and do my shopping and things.

'At the moment it is still early days but she is happy enough and is fortunate enough to have plenty of company. We take each day as it comes.'

Marian, aged 66

'After Mum developed dementia she became increasingly dependent on me and very forgetful. She accused me of stealing from her and I was very upset about this at the time.

'I felt I was chasing my tail most of the time. My own family was taking second place the more I was doing for her. I was working full-time and found it very difficult to cope. There was little help until my brother, Bill, contacted the Adams Agency. We had to pay privately for this. They sent someone in to make her a light lunch and help her. However, she sometimes wouldn't let them in.

'I wanted to have her at my house but she wanted to take the bus home – something she had never done from my house. If asked where she lived, she would name a part of the city she lived in before she married.

'Finally, I took her for an assessment. I was told to put her into somewhere for respite and to find somewhere for her on a permanent basis. We soon found a residential home nearby.'

Anne, aged 68

'My husband's whole personality has changed. He used to be a positive, happy, outgoing person but is now a withdrawn, miserable, grumpy man who is frightened of everything. He has always loved to talk and was renowned for his communication skills. I would say he was born to talk – sometimes too much!

'We are now like two foreigners living together, neither of whom can understand the other one! We have been told that his disease is not following the normal pattern – it has severely affected his language skills but he can still find his way around on the train by himself.

'One of our sons has been so supportive, whereas the other has just totally ignored us – he doesn't even phone! We have been through a lot in our lives, like business problems and divorce, but nothing can compare to the despair and anger I feel with this disease. Unlike cancer or other awful diseases, this changes the whole character of the person.'

How to stay positive

It sounds like a bit of a contradiction, doesn't it? How do you stay positive when you have been diagnosed with a disease which, as yet, has no cure? The answer is that you have to – it is the best way of coping. If you lose that positive attitude, you increase the risk of developing depression which can be hard to come out of.

However, it's easier said than done. So here are some tips. Firstly, let go of the blame. Reading the many newspaper reports on suggested causes and what we could have done in the past will not help and is not a proactive way of living your life. You can live a healthy life, keep your mind active and eat all the right foods, but unfortunately this will not totally rule out your chances of developing Alzheimer's. Don't blame yourself and don't blame the advice you were given or not given – just forget blaming altogether.

Instead, laugh. Yes, laugh. Keep your sense of humour or develop a stronger one. Really, you do have a lot to laugh about. Next time you ask someone what day it is only to discover you have already asked this at least 10 times, laugh. View it as funny.

If you can't find the dishes because they are in the washing machine – laugh. Why not? If you did something as silly as this and you didn't have Alzheimer's you would laugh, so why not now?

Take each day as it comes and ensure that you enjoy life. Many of us go through life with plans for what we will do in the future but never get round to it. If health and circumstance allow it, do these things. Enjoy life and appreciate what you have got.

Don't predict the future. You can't and shouldn't. Alzheimer's is too hard to predict and does not follow a certain path. Stick to the present. Be ready for the changes which may occur but don't focus on them.

Most of all, remember that Alzheimer's is part of your life but not all of your life. Make changes that will allow you to continue enjoying life and aim to get as much out of every day as you can.

Summing Up

- Plan for the future but don't focus on it. Consider making up an advanced statement.

- Alzheimer's research is severely underfunded but much work is still being done.

- While a cure for Alzheimer's has not yet been found, current research should be viewed as taking us one step closer to this.

- Much research is being conducted into causes and prevention, helping us to understand the whole make-up of the disease.

- Try to stay positive. Keep your sense of humour and aim to enjoy life. Remember that Alzheimer's is only part of your life. Live for today and try to enjoy every little thing.

Help List

Alzheimer's Disease International

64 Great Suffolk Street, London, SE1 0BL
Tel: 020 79810880
info@alz.co.uk
www.alz.co.uk
Alzheimer's Disease International is the umbrella organisation of Alzheimer's associations around the world. It provides statistics and details of research plus advice and support.

Alzheimer's Research Trust

The Stables, Station Road, Great Shelford, Cambridge, CB22 5LR
Tel: 01223 843899
enquiries@alzheimers-research.org.uk
www.alzheimers-research.org.uk
The Alzheimer's Research Trust describes itself as the 'UK's leading research charity for dementia'. As well as funding research, it provides information on Alzheimer's and current research.

Alzheimer's Scotland

22 Drumsheugh Gardens, Edinburgh, EH3 7RN
Tel: 0808 8083000 (helpline)
alzheimer@alzscot.org
www.alzscot.org
Alzheimer's Scotland serves people with Alzheimer's in Scotland and also carers, family and professional organisations. They have volunteers who work with people in day centres and drop-in centres and provide many other services including a 24-hour helpline. They have branches throughout Scotland, some of which provide a home support service. They are an excellent point of contact for information on welfare rights and for support.

Alzheimer's Society

Devon House, 58 St Katherine's Way, London, E1W 1JX
Tel: 0845 3000336 (helpline)
enquiries@alzheimers.org.uk
www.alzheimers.org.uk
The Alzheimer's Society aims to improve the quality of life for people affected by Alzheimer's. With approximately 25,000 members ranging from people with dementia to carers and health professionals, it is often the first point of contact for information on Alzheimer's, services available and for keeping you up-to-date. Its Internet discussion forum Talking Point allows you to chat with others about Alzheimer's and how you are feeling.

American Psychological Association

www.apa.org/releases/memory_training.html
Website which gives more information on memory training, especially for Alzheimer's sufferers.

Carers Allowance Unit

Palatine House, Lancaster Road, Preston, Lancashire, PR1 1HB
Tel: 01253 856123
cau.customer-services@dwp.gsi.gov.uk
Contact for details of the Carer's Allowance. See the Directgov website for details.

Dementia Research Centre

Box 16, The National Hospital for Neurology and Neurosurgery, Queen Square, London, WC1N 3BG
Tel: 020 78298773
www.dementia.ion.ucl.ac.uk
The Dementia Research Centre is one of the UK's leading centres for clinical research into dementia. It also trials new drugs to slow the progression of Alzheimer's.

DirectGov

www.direct.gov.uk

This is the government website for people looking for information on benefits they may be due, including carers. Easy to navigate, it has information leaflets to download, details on rates and printable claims forms.

Disability Benefits Helpline

Warbreck House, Warbreck Hill, Blackpool, Lancashire, FY2 0YE
Tel: 08457 123 456 (helpline)
dcpu.customer-services@dwp.gsi.gov.uk
See the directgov website for details on the Disability Living Allowance and the Attendance Allowance or contact the helpline for more information.

For Dementia

6 Camden High Street, London, NW1 0JH
Tel: 020 7874 7210
info@fordementia.org.uk
www.fordementia.org.uk
For Dementia provides training for those who work with people with dementia as well as employing Admiral Nurses, specialist dementia nurses who work in the community with families and carers.

Help the Aged/Age Concern

England
York House, 207-221 Pentonville Road, London, N1 9UZ
Tel: 020 7278 1114
info@helptheaged.org.uk
Astral House, 1268 London Road, London SW16 4ER
Tel: 020 8765 7200
Wales
Ty John Pathy, Units 13/14 Neptune Court, Vanguard Way, Cardiff, CF24 5PJ
Tel: 029 2043 1555
enquiries@agecymru.org.uk

Scotland

Causewayside House, 160 Causewayside, Edinburgh, EH9 1PR

Tel: 0845 833 0200

enquiries@ageconcernandhelptheagedscotland.org.uk

Northern Ireland

3 Lower Crescent, Belfast, BT7 1NR

Tel: 02890 230 666

info@ageconcernhelptheagedni.org

www.helptheaged.org.uk; www.ageconcern.org.uk

On 1 April 2009, Help the Aged and Age Concern England joined together to form Age Concern and Help the Aged. The new organisation campaigns for the rights of older people, provides advice and support, develops services for older people and supports research which could aid older people.

Helping Hands

Arrow House, 8-9 Church Street, Alcester, Warwickshire, B49 5AJ

Tel: 0808 180 9455

enquiries@helpinghandshomecare.co.uk

www.helpinghandshomecare.co.uk

Helping Hands is an agency which provides live-in care specialists for people who want to remain in their own homes.

Lancet

www.thelancet.com

Website for *The Lancet*, Britain's leading medical journal, which has information on memory training.

Princess Royal Trust for Carers

Unit 14, Bourne Court, Southend Road, Woodford Green, Essex, IG8 8HD

Tel: 0844 800 4361

info@carers.org

www.carers.org

The Princess Royal Trust for Carers is one of the largest providers of carer support services. There are 144 carers' centres throughout the UK providing information, advice and support to carers.

Royal College of Psychiatrists

17 Belgrave Square, London, SW1X 8PG
Tel: 020 72352351
rcpsych@rcpsych.ac.uk
www.rcpsych.ac.uk
The Royal College of Psychiatrists' website contains some excellent information on Alzheimer's and treatments.

Scottish Dementia Working Group

81 Oxford Street, Glasgow, G5 9EP
Tel: 0141 418 3939
sdwg@alzscot.org
www.sdwg.org.uk
The Scottish Dementia Working Group is an independent group run by, and with membership open to, people with dementia. It campaigns for people with dementia, seeking to improve services and attitudes.